DEDICATED
TO ALL OF THOSE GROWNUPS
WHO, AS CHILDREN,
DIED IN THE ARMS
OF COMPULSORY EDUCATION.

Albert Cullum

THE GERANIUM ON THE WINDOW SILL JUST DIED BUT TEACHER YOU WENT RIGHT ON

A Harlin Quist Book

BY ALBERT CULLUM

PUBLISHED BY HARLIN QUIST, INCORPORATED
PUBLISHED SIMULTANEOUSLY IN THE BRITISH COMMONWEALTH BY QUIST PUBLISHING, LIMITED
LIBRARY OF CONGRESS CATALOG CARD NUMBER: 75-141525
SBN/TRADE: 8252-0063-6/LIBRARY: 8252-0064-4
TEXT AND ILLUSTRATIONS COPYRIGHT©1971 BY HARLIN QUIST, INCORPORATED
ALL RIGHTS RESERVED
COLOR SEPARATIONS BY GRAPHOTEX
PRINTED IN GERMANY BY J. FINK DRUCKEREI

PUBLISHERS' NOTE:

At a time when there is much communication about the lack of communication,
we publish THE GERANIUM ON THE WINDOW SILL JUST DIED
BUT TEACHER YOU WENT RIGHT ON — with joy.
Like a simple introduction to Permutations and Combinations
(A and B, A and C, A and D, B and C, B and D . . .),
the author and the illustrators speak.
They speak to children as from children; they speak to adults as from adults.
They are adults speaking to adults and to children from their own childhoods;
they tell of the hearts of children now . . .
Take this book to yourself. Remember how you felt,
small and awkward and powerless, in a world of teachers and parents and principals.
It reminds you that children still feel that way.
Give the book to the children.
It will evoke delighted recognition — and, even, reassurance:
"I'm not the only one who thinks that way!"

It's September again
— the time of jumping when you call,
doing cartwheels for you,
nodding yes.
It's September again
— standing on my head for you,
leaping high,
hoping to please.
It's September again
— taking your tests,
finding my lost pencil,
losing ground.
It's September again
— hiding behind my reading book,
breathing quietly,
afraid!

"Good boys and good girls always listen.
To learn, we must listen.
We must listen all the time.
Good boys and girls never talk,
but they always listen.
We should listen and listen and listen!"

To you, teacher,
and your words, your words, your words.
Your words, your words, your words,
your words!

Classroom corners—stale and pale!
Classroom corners—cobweb covered!
Classroom corners—spooky and lonely!

Teacher, let me dance in your classroom corner!
Let the outside world in!

You're so proud of your shiny new car.
You're so proud of your new color hair,
your vacation tan,
and your nice clean blackboards.
I sit in the third row, last seat.
Teacher, are you ever proud of me?

Teacher, let me swim in a puddle,
let me race a cloud in the sky,
let me build a house without walls.
But most of all,
let me laugh at nothing things.

I couldn't help it!
I tried to hold it back! I tried hard!
I couldn't help it that I pooped!
Everyone giggled except you.
You gave me a dirty look.
Why didn't you smile if you've forgotten how to laugh?
At least until the redness went out of my face.

On the mornings you tell us about the night before,
you're like one of us.
The dress you bought,
or a movie you saw,
or a strange sound you heard.
You're a good storyteller, teacher, honest!
And that's when I never have to be excused.

I have a messy desk,
I have milk money that rolls,
I have a lazy pencil,
a book that won't open,
a mouth that whispers.
I have a zipper that doesn't want to,
homework that won't work,
and a hand that throws crayons.
I have a shirt that's out,
shoelaces that won't tie.
And sometimes I wet my pants—
but never on purpose.

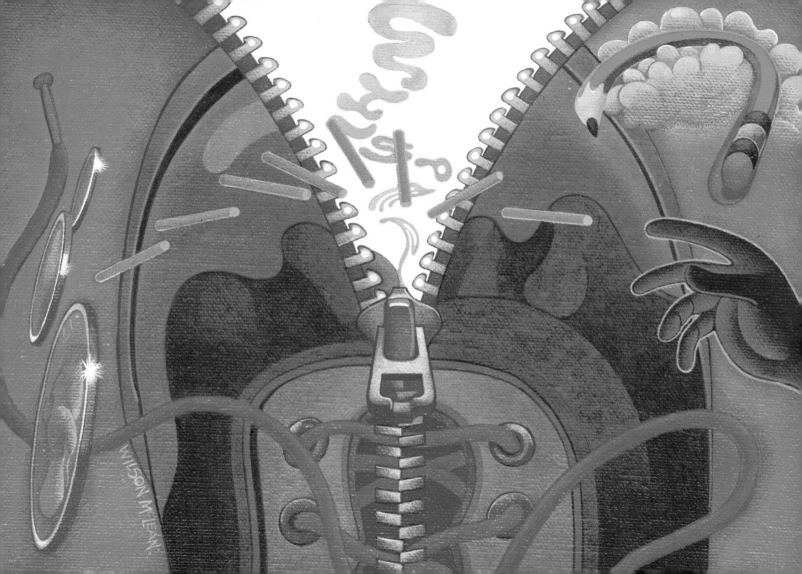

Oh, clean school wall, hallway wall, hold me up!
She pushed me out.
Oh, quiet school wall, hallway wall,
she pushed me hard.
Oh, alone school wall, hallway wall, be my friend! . . .

No, Sister, we didn't drop it on purpose!
Yes, Sister, it was an accident!

Yes, Sister!
Yes, Sister!
Yes, Sister, we will never be careless again, Sister!

No, Sister!
No, Sister, we didn't mean to be silly.
(We didn't even mean to be born!)

Yes, Sister!
Yes, Sister!
Oh my God, we are heartily sorry for having offended Thee!

You, my dear teacher,
you who tell me my thoughts are wrong,
you who are so neat and strong,
you so strict and proper and lukewarm,
you who tell me that I <u>can't</u> and that I <u>shouldn't</u>!
You, you—
<u>who</u> <u>are</u> <u>you</u>?

The day had become like half a night,
but you put the classroom lights on.
The wind blew the papers off your desk,
but you just closed the window.
The trees waved, like they were calling out to us . . .
"Turn to page 67," you said.

You don't have to call me to your desk.
You don't have to whisper "For shame! For shame!"
You don't have to send me out in the hallway.
Just tell me that my zipper is open!

Your perfume covers the whole room,
but I don't like its smell.
You always tell me that I'm the smartest,
but sometimes I wish I were dumb.
Teacher, please don't be so nice to me!
Do I <u>have</u> to be your favorite?

Don't you see my rainbow, teacher?
Don't you see all the colors?
I know that you're mad at me.
I know that you said to color the cherries red and the leaves green.
I guess I shouldn't have done it backwards.
But, teacher, don't you see my rainbow?
Don't you see all the colors?
Don't you see me?

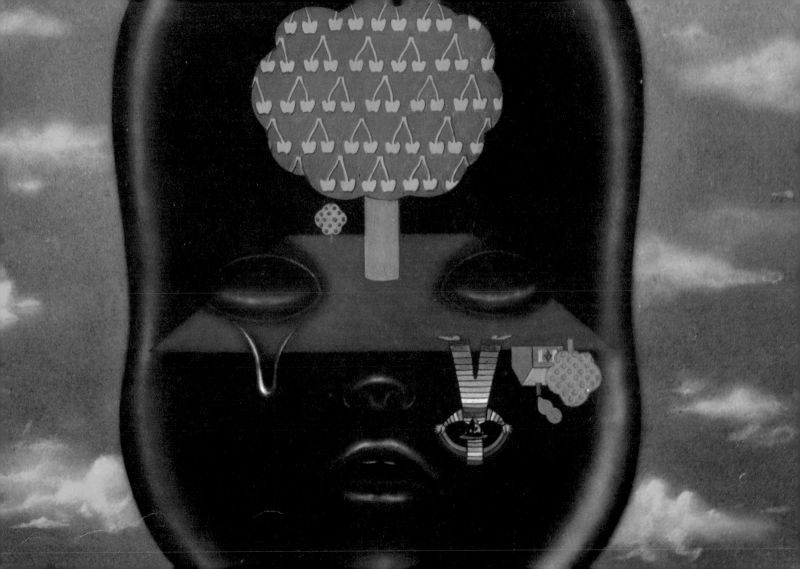

When you don't like me, teacher,
I feel the whole world sees me in wrinkled pants.
Or in my underwear with no pants on.
I know I'm not very smart.
And sometimes I laugh when I shouldn't.
But I don't want to go home with you not liking me.
Please!
Choose me to wash the blackboards at three o'clock!

I was good at everything
—honest, everything!—
until I started being here with you.
I was good at laughing,
playing dead,
being king!
Yeah, I was good at everything!
But now I'm only good at everything
on Saturdays and Sundays . . .

Yes, Mr. Principal,
I will sing your song.

Cheep, cheep,
you are always right.

Cheep, cheep,
you are very great.

Cheep, cheep,
you are God!

Cheep, cheep,
cheep, cheep . . . <u>cheep</u>.

I'm so quiet sitting in the first row, first seat.
I feel you like me.
I mind, and I am never late.
Do you like me?
I always do all of my homework,
and I gave you the biggest valentine of all.
Do you like me?
Sometimes I'm scared of you though.
The way you look, the way you smile.
But that's when you like me best of all—
when I'm scared.

You talk funny when you talk to the principal.
Or when the teacher next door borrows some paper.
And when my mother comes to see you,
you talk funny.
Why don't you talk to them like you talk to us?

It was great seeing you on Saturday.
You said "hello" to me in the center of town.
Even after you passed me, I heard your "hello."
Teacher, does this mean that you like me
and that I'm going to get promoted?

Sometimes I don't pee straight.
And Jimmy next in line always reports me.
I guess Jimmy pees straight all the time.
Is that why he's your favorite?

I want you to come to my house,
and yet I don't.
You're so important,
but our screendoor has a hole in it.
And my mother has no fancy cake to serve.
I want you to come to my house, teacher,
and yet I don't.
My brother chews with his mouth wide open,
and sometimes my dad burps.
I wish I could trust you enough, teacher,
to invite you to my house.

Teacher, give me back my "I"—!
You promised, teacher,
you promised if I was good you'd give it back.
You have so many "I's" in the top drawer of your desk.
You wouldn't miss mine.

Where is my place in your puzzle, teach?
Do I fit?
Or am I one piece too many?
Tell me for real, teach!
I <u>know</u> there's no room for me on your bulletin board,
but do I have a place in your puzzle?

The robins sang and sang and sang,
but teacher you went right on.
The last bell sounded the end of the day,
but teacher you went right on.
The geranium on the window sill just died,
but teacher you went right on.

Teacher, I guess you won.

"Good morning, class!
Today I will prepare you for the future.
Listen carefully,
and don't interrupt!
Are there any questions? . . .
None?
Good!"

Teacher, come on outside!
I'll race you to the seesaw!
No, you won't fall off!
I'll show you how!
Don't be afraid, teacher.
Grab my hand and follow me.
You can learn all over again! . . .

THE ILLUSTRATORS: J. K. Lambert   page   6

Nicole Claveloux   9

Jean Seisser   11

Lorraine Fox   13

John Alcorn   15

Philippe Weisbecker   17

Richard Amsel   19

Wilson McLean   21

Guy Billout   23

Jaqueline Duheme   25

Jacques Rozier   27

Bernard d'Andrea   29

Guillermo Mordillo   31

Catherine Loeb   33

Georges Lacroix   35

Michel Gay   37

Reynold Ruffins   39

Jean-Jacques Loup   41

Franklin Luke   43

Henri Galeron   45

Robert Andrew Parker   47

Bernard Bonhomme   49

Claude Lapointe   51

Patrick Couratin   53

Nestor de Arzadun   55

Alan E. Cober   57

Stanley Mack   59

Norman Adams   61

Cover and title page illustrations

Philippe Weisbecker